Author: Kätriin Kaldaru
ISBN HARDBACK: 978-9916-79-720-4
ISBN PAPERBACK: 978-9916-79-721-1
ISBN EBOOK: 978-9916-79-722-8

Glistening Hush of Dawn

The first light creeps, a golden hue,
Whispers of night fade, soft and true.
Birds begin to sing, their melody bright,
A canvas ignites, from darkness to light.

Morning dew glistens, a diamond's grace,
Nature awakens, each petal, each face.
Clouds gently drift, like dreams in the sky,
As soft breezes weave, where the shadows lie.

The world holds its breath, in tranquil embrace,
Awakening hearts, in this sacred space.
Hope blooms anew, in the still of the morn,
Each moment a gift, as the day is reborn.

Silken Chill

The evening air breathes a silken chill,
Whispers of winter, so calm and still.
Stars twinkle softly, like distant eyes,
Glistening dreams weave through midnight skies.

Frost-kissed branches, a lacework adorn,
Nature's quiet splendor, in silence is born.
Moonlight embraces, the world wrapped in white,
A hush over valleys, a blanket of night.

Echoes of shadows, dance on the ground,
In this peaceful moment, pure magic is found.
The world slows its pace, in the still of the air,
Each breath a secret, a silken prayer.

Ethereal Chill in Stillness

In twilight's embrace, a chill settles deep,
Under the watch of the stars as they peep.
The air holds a shimmer, a mysterious grace,
Time drifts like clouds, in this quiet space.

Frosted whispers cradle the night,
A ghostly introspection, tranquil and white.
Moments waltz softly, in a slow, tender glide,
While shadows retreat, where dreams often hide.

Echoing silence, a gentle refrain,
Nature's sweet lullaby, soft as the rain.
Each breath a reflection, a calming embrace,
As dreams take their flight, in the stillness of space.

Breath of the Arctic Spirit

The breath of the Arctic calls through the night,
Whispers of wonder, both wild and bright.
Snowflakes dance softly, like feathers that fall,
Nature's own canvas, a magnificent call.

Beneath the pale moon, the stillness retains,
The secrets of ages, through snow, wind, and rains.
Mountains like sentinels, watch from afar,
Guardians of dreams, 'neath the Northern Star.

Icebergs drift gently, like thoughts in the sea,
Hauntingly lovely, forever to be.
The spirit of frost, in each whispering breath,
Eternal, unyielding, beyond life and death.

Chill in the Whisper

In the stillness, shadows creep,
Softly cradling dreams that sleep.
A breeze that whispers through the trees,
Brings secrets carried on the freeze.

Frosty tendrils touch the air,
Nature's breath, a gentle scare.
Each moment wrapped in silver haze,
Time pauses in this winter maze.

Stars blink down on silent ground,
Where echoes of the past are found.
The world stands still, a breath held tight,
In the chill of the velvet night.

Icy Echoes of Silence

Frozen whispers glide on air,
Carrying tales of winter's care.
A quiet realm, a frosty shroud,
Where solitude whispers aloud.

Footsteps crunch on icy trails,
As nature sighs, the moment pales.
Every flake, a ghostly dance,
In this vast, enchanting expanse.

Moonlight bathes the world in white,
Painting shadows, soft and slight.
Echoes linger, rich and deep,
In the quest for dreams we keep.

Breath of Winter's Veil

Winter's breath, a frosty sigh,
Cloaks the land as night drifts by.
Softly wrapped in a quilt of snow,
Nature whispers secrets low.

The chill dances in the trees,
Echoing like a gentle tease.
Stars above in silent grace,
Kiss the earth with a silvery trace.

Each heartbeat resonates the calm,
Woven deep in winter's balm.
Through the stillness, dreams arise,
Wrapped within the starry skies.

Shivers on the Wind

A gust of air, sharp and clear,
Brings the frost that draws us near.
In every shiver, stories weave,
Of warmth and hope that we believe.

Beneath the grey, the world stands cold,
Yet in its heart, a flame of gold.
Through whispered winds, our spirits soar,
In search of warmth forevermore.

A canvas white, untouched and bright,
Awakens dreams of pure delight.
As shivers dance upon the skin,
We find the warmth that lies within.

A Symphony of Stillness

In twilight's grace, the shadows play,
Whispers of quiet at the close of day.
Stars awaken in a velvet sky,
Silent melodies drift softly by.

Moonlight dances on the gentle stream,
Every ripple holds a sacred dream.
Nature's sigh, a tranquil refrain,
In the stillness, peace we gain.

Leaves flutter down with the evening breeze,
Wrapped in warmth, lost in memories.
The night hums with a hidden song,
In its embrace, we all belong.

Crickets serenade the darkened land,
Each note is woven like grains of sand.
Time suspends its hurried race,
In this quiet, we find our place.

So let the night unfold its art,
A symphony soothing the restless heart.
In each moment, we find the way,
Through the stillness, night turns to day.

White Silence Upon the Cheek

Snowflakes descend like whispered dreams,
Blanketing the world in silver gleams.
A hush falls softly on the ground,
In this stillness, beauty is found.

Each flake unique, a gentle kiss,
Covering the earth in frosted bliss.
Winter's breath paints the landscape white,
Transforming day into ethereal night.

Trees wear crowns of crystal frost,
In this silence, nothing is lost.
Footsteps fade in the winter glow,
A tranquil moment wrapped in snow.

Stars peek through a quilt of clouds,
The night wraps around, serenity shrouds.
In the cold, a warmth ignites,
A bond forged in these silent nights.

White silence lingers, a sacred space,
Embracing all in its soft embrace.
Let us cherish the calm we seek,
In winter's arms, life feels unique.

The Echo of Winter's Lullaby

In the quiet of a frosty eve,
Winter sings, and we believe.
A lullaby wrapped in snow,
To the heart, warmth it will bestow.

Whispers weave through barren trees,
Carried along by a shivering breeze.
The night blankets the world in gray,
In its embrace, worries sway away.

Moonlight glimmers on a frozen lake,
Crystals shimmer, as dreams awake.
The echoes dance in a cool embrace,
A wishful sigh, time slows its pace.

Cradle the night, hold it near,
Every whisper holds a memory dear.
In each soft note, hopes arise,
Beneath this canvas of starlit skies.

As dawn approaches, dreams take flight,
With every shadow fading from sight.
The echo of winter will remain,
A lullaby soft, in our hearts, it's ingrained.

Icicles of Memory Hang Low

Icicles dangle from the eaves,
Hanging like secrets, stories we weave.
Glinting in sunlight, crystal bright,
Each one holds a moment, pure delight.

Nostalgia drips in the winter air,
Whispers of warmth linger everywhere.
Frozen in time, memories unfold,
A tapestry woven with threads of gold.

Snow-laden branches sigh with grace,
Stoic witness to a weathered face.
Each shed tear turned to ice, it seems,
Frosty reminders of lost dreams.

Beneath the chill, a fire ignites,
Reviving the warmth of cherished nights.
Icicles melt with the sun's embrace,
In every drop flows a loving trace.

So we gather memories, cold yet clear,
Holding them close, year after year.
Icicles of memory, shining and low,
In winter's heart, our affirmations grow.

Glistening Hues of Breath

In morning's light, a whisper glows,
Colors dance where the soft wind blows.
Shimmering shades of life's embrace,
Each breath a brushstroke, a fleeting trace.

With every sigh, the world takes form,
A canvas bright with hues so warm.
Nature's palette, vivid and clear,
Awakens hope, dispelling fear.

The sun ignites the sky's deep blue,
As dreams awaken, fresh and true.
A tapestry of moments spun,
In glistening hues, the day's begun.

Frosted Secrets of the Dawn

In twilight's grasp, the frost took hold,
Secrets whispered, soft and cold.
Each crystal spark a tale to tell,
Of night's embrace, where wonders dwell.

The world adorned in silver light,
A silent spell, enchanting sight.
Nature's breath, a gentle sigh,
In frosted dreams, the spirits fly.

Awakening earth, in shimmers bright,
Unveils the wonders hidden from sight.
As dawn unfolds with tender grace,
The frozen night begins to chase.

The Stillness of Winter's Kiss

Snowflakes drift in a tranquil dance,
Each one cradled in winter's trance.
The world holds breath, as moments pause,
In stillness, find the heart's true cause.

Nights adorned with a silken shroud,
Whispers soft beneath the cloud.
Crimson embers, warm the air,
In winter's kiss, we find our care.

Time slows down with nature's art,
Revealing peace within the heart.
With every flake, a story told,
In winter's grip, we feel consoled.

Hushed Murmurs in Ice

In the silence, whispers glide,
Through frozen dreams, where secrets hide.
Ice-bound echoes of the soul,
In a world where the stillness is whole.

Veils of frost, like tender sighs,
Painting stories under gray skies.
Each moment caught in frigid grace,
In hushed murmurs, we find our place.

The chill embraces, a gentle press,
Hushed murmurs bring a sense of rest.
Winter's breath, both soft and fierce,
In icy realms, our hearts immerse.

Glacial Poems of the Void

In the silence, whispers freeze,
Echoes dance on frozen seas.
Winds carry tales of ages past,
In the void where shadows cast.

Stars shimmer in the endless night,
A stillness drapes the world in white.
Crystals form on the barren ground,
In the stillness, truths abound.

Time stands still in icy grace,
Each breath lost in this silent space.
Frozen dreams in the pallid glow,
Awakening where none dare go.

Beneath the surface, secrets lie,
In the heart of the frost, a sigh.
Memories locked in winter's hold,
A story of the empty and bold.

Yet within this chilling realm,
An ancient force begins to helm.
Through the ice, a pulse that's true,
Yearning for warmth, breaking through.

Breath from the Icebound Heart

From the depths of winter's sigh,
A heartbeat whispers, soft and shy.
Frigid air wraps 'round the soul,
In the stillness, we feel whole.

Frosted branches cradle dreams,
In the night, a quiet gleam.
Nature's breath, a soft lament,
In the cold, our warmth is spent.

Echoes of a lingering past,
Between the snowflakes, shadows cast.
Yearning for a touch, a start,
A journey sparked from icebound heart.

With every pulse, the cold retreats,
While silence sings in whispered beats.
In glacial chambers, love's ignite,
Amidst the dark, the purest light.

Together we, in frigid air,
Find solace, entwined in prayer.
For even in the harshest freeze,
Love's breath brings forth the soul's ease.

Enigmas in the Winter Air

In the depths of silent night,
Mysterious forms dance in the light.
Voices drift on the frosty breeze,
Whispers caught in frozen trees.

Stars shimmering with untold tales,
Beneath the weight of winter's veils.
Questions linger in the chill,
In the stillness, hearts do thrill.

Footprints left in the glistening snow,
Guiding paths where shadows flow.
Secrets buried in layers deep,
Echo in dreams that softly creep.

A tapestry of frost is spun,
Veiling truths until the sun.
In every heartbeat, a riddle plays,
In winter's grasp, the mind decays.

Yet from the mists of cold despair,
Hope rises in the winter air.
For every enigma, a spark remains,
A warmth ignited as daylight gains.

Veil of Subzero Dreams

Morning mist in shrouded gray,
Cloaks the world in soft dismay.
Frozen moments gently weave,
A tapestry we can believe.

Underneath the crystal skies,
Subtle wishes in silence lie.
Hopes entwined in bitter sweet,
In the frozen pulse, we meet.

Each snowflake a wish unmade,
Gliding down, a soft cascade.
In the whispers of the deep,
Veils of dreams gently keep.

Frosted echoes paint the night,
With shadows dancing, pure and bright.
A realm where imagination sings,
In the silence, endless springs.

Through layers thick, the heart finds air,
Breath of warmth amidst despair.
In subzero truths, we trust,
Finding beauty in the rust.

Shades of Winter's Veil

Whispers glide through frosty air,
A blanket woven without care.
Trees wear coats of shimmering white,
A serene stillness reigns the night.

Footsteps crunch on frozen ground,
In this silence, peace is found.
Moonlight dances on the ice,
Nature's beauty, pure and nice.

Hues of blue in twilight gleam,
In chilly shadows, dreams do stream.
Softly falls the drifting snow,
A winter's tale in whispers flow.

Branches bow with heavy load,
On this cold, enchanted road.
Colors muted, whispers blend,
As the veil of winter descends.

Echoes of a world asleep,
In cold arms the Earth will keep.
Through the night, the stars will shine,
In winter's shade, all hearts align.

Celestial Frost at the Dawn of Time

Stars awaken in the sky,
As dawn paints its colors high.
Frosted fields begin to glow,
In the light, a gentle flow.

Veils of mist drift soft and slow,
Kissing earth with tender show.
Crystals catch the golden hue,
In every breath, a moment new.

Nature stirs in quiet grace,
In the dawn, a sacred space.
Quiet marvels wrapped in light,
Frosty dreams that feel so right.

The sun begins its warm embrace,
Chasing shadows, leaving trace.
Every glimmer tells a tale,
In this frost, where whispers sail.

Time unravels with each ray,
An ethereal ballet.
Moments lost in magical skies,
Where frost and sunlight softly ties.

Chilling Harmony of the Evening

Night descends with chill embrace,
Stars emerge and take their place.
Cool winds weave through branches bare,
In the hush, a whispered prayer.

The moon reflects on frozen streams,
Painting silver where it beams.
Notes of silence fill the air,
In the dark, a soothing care.

Shadows dance on warming glow,
Where the secrets of night flow.
Crickets sing their soothing sound,
In this harmony that's profound.

Frosty breath upon the dawn,
Hints of warmth already drawn.
Nature rests yet feels alive,
In this twilight, hearts will thrive.

A symphony of peace unfolds,
In the deep, the night enfolds.
Every star a story tells,
In the chilling harmony, it dwells.

Enigmatic Whispers of the Frost

Softly wrapped in frosty night,
Mysteries cloaked in silver light.
Whispers carried on the breeze,
Secrets hidden, heart's unease.

The world beneath a crystal sheet,
Echoes of the past repeat.
Footprints fade in sparkling snow,
Paths unknown where shadows go.

In the stillness, tales reside,
In the frost, the dreams abide.
Each breath fogs the quiet space,
Nature's touch, a soft embrace.

Underneath the starlit dome,
Whispers beckon us to roam.
Frosted branches, whispers sway,
Guiding spirits lost in play.

Every flake, a story told,
In each gleam, a vision bold.
Through the night, the whispers glide,
In the frost, our dreams do bide.

Frosted Thoughts and Glistening Fears

In the dawn of winter's light,
A frosted breath begins to bite.
Thoughts hang like icicles bright,
Glistening fears take silent flight.

Winds whisper secrets in the trees,
Chasing shadows with brittle ease.
Each step creaks beneath my dreams,
Caught in a web of chilled extremes.

The world dims under a velvet gray,
Frosted thoughts lead me astray.
Wrapped in layers to hide from sight,
Yet the heart warms at winter's night.

Beneath the surface, stories sleep,
Glistening fears linger deep.
The sun retreats, the cold draws near,
In the silence, I face my fear.

With each breath, a crystal sigh,
Frosted thoughts, I let them fly.
In the beauty of this frozen sphere,
I find the strength to persevere.

The Stillness of Snow

White blankets cover the worn ground,
In silence, beauty can be found.
The stillness rests like a gentle vow,
A tranquil moment, here and now.

Trees stand tall in their crystal attire,
Branches adorned, a sight to inspire.
In the hush, the world seems to hold,
Secrets of winter, silent and bold.

Animals hide in their cozy lairs,
While snowflakes dance in the frosty airs.
Every flake unique like a whispered prayer,
The stillness wraps life in a soft snare.

Footprints fade, a memory lost,
In the quiet, we ponder the cost.
Nature's embrace, a gentle thaw,
The stillness of snow—peaceful awe.

As night falls and stars softly gleam,
We find solace in this winter dream.
In the calm, our hearts align,
The stillness of snow, pure and divine.

Crystal Clear Lamentations

In the winter's grasp, I quietly weep,
Frosted whispers, secrets I keep.
Crystal droplets form on the pane,
Reflecting the world, sorrow and pain.

Each flake a memory, lost in the breeze,
Falling softly like whispered pleas.
In the stillness, my heart feels the weight,
Crystal clear thoughts of lingering fate.

The trees wear their coats of icy dread,
While silence echoes what's left unsaid.
Lamentations dance on the edge of dreams,
In a world that's frozen, nothing redeems.

Yet within this cold, a flicker exists,
Hope among shadows, a warmth that persists.
Through crystal corridors, I find my voice,
In lamentations, I must rejoice.

Though the winter season brings a chill,
My heart remains steadfast, a steadfast will.
For every cry turned to shimmering lace,
Holds the promise of warmth in its embrace.

A Hush Within the Ice

Beneath the surface of the frozen lake,
Lies a hush that the cold winds make.
Memories linger in glacial tones,
Whispered secrets trapped in frozen bones.

Footsteps echo on a snow-white ground,
In the silence, solace can be found.
The world slows down, a gentle sigh,
A hush within the ice, where echoes lie.

Nature's quiet wraps around my soul,
As I wander through this spellbound whole.
Each breath becomes a frosted gift,
In the stillness, I find my spirit lift.

Crystal formations speak tales of old,
A narrative wrapped in winter's cold.
Within this cocoon, a tranquility reigns,
A hush within the ice, as peace remains.

Though winter's grip may feel so tight,
The hush reveals beauty in the night.
In icy stillness, the heart can find,
A world reborn, with love entwined.

Whispering Winds of the Cold

The winds whisper tales, softly they speak,
With breath of winter, the world feels bleak.
Trees bow low, in a chilling embrace,
Nature's own secrets, time can't erase.

Frosted whispers dance, beneath the pale moon,
Carrying dreams that wane all too soon.
Echoes of silence, in dusk's tender hold,
Every sigh a memory, a story retold.

Snowflakes descend, with grace they fall,
Painting the earth in a shimmering shawl.
Each flake a whisper, unique in its flight,
Kissing the landscape, soft as the night.

Winter's breath lingers, in moments gone by,
A tranquil symphony beneath the gray sky.
Eyes closed in solace, hearts intertwined,
With the whispering winds, peace we will find.

In the cold's gentle hug, we find our way,
Guided by warmth, though the skies turn gray.
Through frozen paths where dreams gently unfold,
We walk hand in hand, as the winds grow bold.

A Symphony in Frost

Strings of ice twinkle, in twilight's embrace,
Nature's orchestra plays, in this wintry space.
Each note a flake, as it drifts to the ground,
An echo of silence, in beauty profound.

A crescendo rises, soft and serene,
Wrapped in the stillness, a magical scene.
Whispers of snow in a hushed lullaby,
Swaying like dreams that kiss the night sky.

Frothy white melodies, glisten and gleam,
Carried on breezes, like whispers of a dream.
A bow drawn across, the heartstrings alight,
In harmony found, in the cool of the night.

The trees sway gently, keeping the time,
Nature's ensemble, in rhythm and rhyme.
With every soft step, we dance through the freeze,
Lost in the symphony, a moment to seize.

As dawn breaks the silence, in colors anew,
A masterpiece painted, in vibrant hues.
A symphony in frost, across fields will go,
A tale of the winter, in hearts we'll bestow.

Shattered Silence of the Snow

Silence engulfs, a blanket so white,
Yet whispers of winter break forth in the night.
With every soft footprint, we tread on the hush,
In the shattered silence, the world starts to blush.

The air bites gently, crisp and so clear,
Carrying secrets that linger near.
In stillness we wander, beneath the pale glow,
Embracing the magic, of the soft, falling snow.

Branches creak softly, the weight they do bear,
Wrapped in white wonders, beyond all compare.
Nature's own canvas, a pristine delight,
In the shattered silence, a symphony bright.

The moon softly beams, casting shadows so long,
In this frozen moment, we sing winter's song.
Each glance exchanged holds a warmth so divine,
In the quiet of snow, our souls intertwine.

As dawn approaches, the stillness will wane,
But echoes of silence will always remain.
In the heart of the winter, we found our own flow,
In the beauty that thrives, in the shattered snow.

Ethereal Frost upon the Lips

Ethereal frost kisses, the edges of dreams,
Whispers of chill glide, like delicate streams.
Softly it beckons, the night in repose,
Caressing our thoughts as the twilight sows.

Upon trembling lips, the frost finds its place,
A shimmer of starlight, a silvery trace.
Every sweet breath, holds a magic untold,
Woven in whispers, the night's gentle hold.

The world glimmers softly, a crystalline choir,
Echoes of winter, in whispers of fire.
In the dance of the frosty, a tender embrace,
We find the connection, to time and to space.

Wrapped in the stillness, the heart learns to sing,
In the cradle of frost, the love of the spring.
Each moment we share holds the world in its sway,
With ethereal frost, we chase shadows away.

As dawn's gentle fingers, paint gold in the sky,
The frost will disperse, but the love won't say bye.
In our orbit of warmth, forever it grips,
The taste of the winter, ethereal, on lips.

Enshrined in a Veil of Cold

In the hush of winter's night,
Silence wraps the world in white.
Stars twinkle with frosty gleam,
Moonlit paths in a frozen dream.

Branches bend under weighty frost,
In the chill, no warmth is lost.
Shadows dance in the silver glow,
Nature whispers secrets slow.

Every breath a cloud of mist,
Moments fade in the night's twist.
Time stands still, as if to wait,
Crystals shimmer, hearts sedate.

Veils of cold, a soft embrace,
Over every color, every space.
In this realm where all is still,
A frigid beauty, pure and shrill.

In the dawn, the world awakes,
Underneath the icy flakes.
Life returns, yet memories hold,
Forever enshrined in a veil of cold.

Whispers Beneath the Snowfall

Snowflakes whisper secrets sweet,
Gentle silence, a soothing beat.
Footsteps muffled, soft and low,
Words are lost in the drifting snow.

In the twilight, shadows blend,
Winter's chill, a faithful friend.
Branches bow with a feathery touch,
Each flake dances, oh so much.

Beneath the blanket, dreams reside,
Frozen hopes, the heart confides.
Every drift a story told,
In whispers soft, the night enfolds.

An echo of laughter lingers long,
Nature hums a silent song.
Through the night, a calm befalls,
Life unfolds beneath the falls.

Morning comes, the sun will rise,
Casting warmth across the skies.
Yet beneath the snow's soft call,
Secrets kept, whispers will enthrall.

The Labyrinth of Frigid Air

In the maze where cold winds wail,
Each twist and turn, a ghostly trail.
Frosted breath hangs in the night,
Guiding souls with pale light.

Echoes bounce off icy walls,
In the depths where silence falls.
Crystalline paths lead astray,
Lost in shadows where spirits play.

Here, the air is thick with dreams,
Frozen thoughts in glistening streams.
Nature's heart beats soft and slow,
In this labyrinth, lost souls flow.

Every pathway holds a tale,
Of wanderers who once set sail.
The chill wraps tight, a lover's hold,
Embracing secrets, stories told.

As dawn breaks, the maze will fade,
Yet memories in frost, remain laid.
Through the glimmer, awash in care,
The passage lives in frigid air.

Chill Whispers in the Air

Whispers float through the icy breeze,
Every snowflake dances with ease.
Voices soft, like a dream's caress,
Frigid songs in winter's dress.

Through the night, a stillness grows,
In the silence, the heart knows.
Chill descends like a gentle sigh,
In the depths where the shadows lie.

Frosted windows, tales obscured,
Nature speaks, and all is stirred.
Every flake carries a wish,
A moment held in winter's swish.

Past the trees, the echoes roam,
Finding solace, a frosty home.
In every whisper, a life is spun,
An icy tale, until it's done.

As dawn approaches, colors blaze,
Yet bye and bye, the chill will stay.
In every heartbeat, every prayer,
Lives the magic, chill whispers in the air.

The Caress of Icy Air

In the hush of winter's breath,
The world is draped in white fashion,
Whispers dance through the trees,
In the silence, I find passion.

Frigid fingers trace my skin,
Each touch sends shivers anew,
Nature's art, both soft and bold,
Painting skies in a wintry hue.

Footsteps crunch on glittering frost,
Echoes of the day's retreat,
Stars blink softly as shadows play,
In the night, all feels complete.

The chill wraps 'round like a shawl,
Keeping warmth close to my heart,
In this moment, I stand tall,
A work of nature's sweetest art.

With breath visible in the air,
I embrace the solitude bright,
In the caress of icy care,
I find solace in the night.

Wisp of Chilling Fog

A shroud of mist creeps on the ground,
It blankets all in ghostly grey,
Obscuring paths that once were clear,
In silence, the shadows sway.

Softly it weaves through trees and stones,
A whisper from the dusk that lingers,
Brushing lightly on my skin,
Gentle touch of nature's fingers.

Each corner hides a hidden tale,
In the wisp, the unseen breathes,
Lost voices echoed through the vale,
In the dance where the fog weaves.

Time feels frozen, moments blend,
In this ethereal embrace,
Lost in dreams, the world transcends,
And in stillness, I find grace.

As dawn approaches, light breaks free,
The fog will yield to sunlit rays,
Yet in my heart, a memory,
Of the chilling fog that sways.

Frostbitten Promises

In the stillness of the night,
Secrets whisper, softly told,
Promises frozen in the air,
Held tight in winter's fold.

Each step crunches with intent,
To follow paths where dreams reside,
In the frost, my heart is bent,
Holding on, with quiet pride.

Beneath the chill, warmth lingers still,
Like embers glowing in the dark,
Frostbitten dreams that time won't kill,
Each flicker ignites a spark.

Underneath this icy glaze,
Life awaits a brighter hue,
With every dawn, hope replays,
In these moments, strong and true.

Frostbitten promises align,
With the beauty of the freeze,
In the heart where love will shine,
Even in the coldest breeze.

Hibernation of the Soul

In the embrace of winter's hold,
The world slips into a deep sleep,
Wrapped in silence, hushed and bold,
In the cocoon of the snow, we keep.

Time seems to pause, shadows blend,
Nature breathes in whispered sighs,
The flicker of life starts to mend,
Beneath the surface, hope still flies.

Buried deep, the dreams reside,
Awaiting spring's warm, tender call,
In this slumber, hearts abide,
Resting gently, through it all.

The soul emerges, fresh and bright,
Like blooms that push through frost-kissed ground,
Hibernation turns to light,
In the warmth, new life is found.

So let the chill envelop me,
In the folds of winter's grace,
For in its depths, I shall see,
The rebirth of my pace.

Chilling Reveries

Whispers of winter touch the air,
Dreams unfold beneath the pale glare.
Snowflakes fall with a silent grace,
In this realm, I find my place.

Frosty breath of the midnight sky,
Echoes of memories drifting by.
In the stillness, thoughts collide,
Chilling reveries, my heart's guide.

Beneath the moon's frosty sheen,
Wonders dance in a world serene.
Cold embraces the peaceful night,
Wrapped in dreams, I feel the light.

Crimson branches, shadows cast,
Moments fleeting, yet held fast.
Nature's canvas, white and wide,
In every flake, secrets hide.

As the dawn begins to break,
Softly curling, I awake.
Chilling visions fade away,
Awaiting warmth of another day.

Tranquility in Icebound Silence

A hush envelops the frozen ground,
Nature slumbers, peace is found.
Crystal landscapes shimmer bright,
Tranquility in the pale moonlight.

Silent woods in a liquid freeze,
Frozen whispers dance on the breeze.
Branches sag under winter's weight,
Time stands still, destiny waits.

Birds bid farewell to the chilly air,
Leaving behind not a single care.
In icebound silence, thoughts run deep,
As the world around me falls asleep.

Footsteps crunch on a snowy trail,
Each echo tells a storied tale.
In the stillness, I sense the calm,
Winter's embrace, a silent balm.

As twilight wraps the earth in gray,
Stars emerge to light the way.
Tranquility found in every glance,
In the quiet night, nature's dance.

The Silence of Frosted Woods

Amidst the trees of frosted white,
Whispers linger in the night.
Every shadow softly speaks,
In the silence, solace seeks.

Muffled sounds beneath the snow,
Footsteps hushed, a gentle flow.
Peaceful glades in moonlit glow,
In frosted woods, my spirit grows.

Branches draped in icy lace,
Nature's beauty finds its space.
Each breath taken feels divine,
In this stillness, I entwine.

Frozen streams like mirrors lie,
Reflecting secrets of the sky.
In this moment, time does bend,
The silence of woods, my faithful friend.

As dawn ignites the winter's chill,
Soft hues awaken, warm and still.
I cherish every whispered word,
In forest depths, my heart is stirred.

A Dance on the Edge of Winter

Footfalls trace a path so clear,
A dance begins as winter nears.
With every twirl, the world spins round,
In the white embrace, joy is found.

Crisp air filled with laughter's sound,
Frosted leaves crunch on the ground.
Caught in nature's frosty reel,
Each step forward, a heart to heal.

Snowflakes twinkle like stars in flight,
Time slows down in the fading light.
Boundless beauty in every glance,
A fleeting moment invites a dance.

Fires burning, warm and bright,
Chasing shadows of the night.
In the chill, our spirits ignite,
A joyous dance, hearts take flight.

As winter's edge begins to fade,
Memories linger, dreams are made.
With every step, the world does sing,
In this dance, we find our spring.

Ethereal Exhalations at Dusk

Whispers of twilight softly greet,
Shadows dance where silence meets.
Colors bleed in fading light,
Promises float into the night.

Gentle breezes carry the sighs,
Crimson blush in the darkening skies.
Stars awaken, twinkling bright,
Guiding dreams through the lunar flight.

Echoes linger in the cool air,
Drawing hearts to a distant prayer.
Moments pass like drifting smoke,
Lingering sweet in every joke.

Silhouettes sway by the old tree,
Crickets sing a calming plea.
Nature hums its soothing song,
In this dusk where we belong.

Time unravels with each breath,
Drawing close life and death.
In this space, we truly find,
Ethereal exhalations bind.

Glacial Dreams in Moonlight

Beneath the moon's soft silver glow,
Frozen dreams in silence flow.
Crystals gleam like distant stars,
Whispers trapped in frozen bars.

The night air carries a gentle chill,
Filling hearts with a sudden thrill.
Shadows stretch across the land,
Painted beauty by nature's hand.

Glacial streams in silver tides,
Flowing secrets where peace abides.
Each breath sings of tranquil grace,
In moonlight's tender, warm embrace.

While the world lies still in sleep,
Ancient secrets, promises keep.
A tapestry woven with time's thread,
In dreams where only hearts dare tread.

Translucent visions, crystal clear,
Hold the essence of all we hold dear.
Awakening hearts in night's gentle glow,
Glacial dreams in moonlight flow.

Frigid Reflections in Time

In the glassy pond's chill sheen,
Frozen echoes of what has been.
Reflections dance in the pale blue,
Whispered stories of me and you.

Time stretches thin like a fraying thread,
Where past and present freely tread.
In the frigid grasp of winter's grasp,
Memories linger in a gentle clasp.

Bare branches reach for the star-filled sky,
In silence, they begin to cry.
While the world turns against the freeze,
Heartbeats echo like gentle pleas.

Each heartbeat writes its timeless page,
In the book of moments, we engage.
Frigid breaths hold warmth inside,
As we navigate the changing tide.

So let us cherish this fleeting play,
In reflections where we wish to stay.
For time is but a fleeting chime,
In these frigid reflections of time.

Crystal Shards of Memory

Scattered across the floor of dreams,
Crystal shards reflect our schemes.
Fragments of joy and whispers of pain,
Each shard holds a timeless refrain.

Through the shards, the past refracts,
Casting shadows, revealing facts.
Moments captured behind the glass,
Echoes of smiles that never pass.

Time's gentle hand shapes each piece,
Crafting memories that never cease.
In every sparkle, a story lies,
Waiting for hearts to empathize.

Fleeting seconds, like shards, may break,
Yet in their splinters, we partake.
Binding threads of love and loss,
In crystal shards, we find our gloss.

With every glance back into the past,
We learn that moments can never last.
Yet through their beauty, we often find,
Crystal shards are a mirror to the mind.

Breath of Crystal Dreams

In twilight's hush, the whispers call,
A dance of light behind the wall.
Each breath a dream, a shimmering sigh,
Where hopes take flight, and shadows fly.

A canvas vast, the stars align,
Embrace the night, let hearts entwine.
With every pulse, a story we weave,
In crystal dreams, we dare believe.

The moonlit path, a silver stream,
Guides wandering souls to what they deem.
In fragile silence, echoes gleam,
A radiant truth, a fervent dream.

The morning sun, a golden ray,
Awakens hearts to greet the day.
In every breath, a chance to start,
To paint the world, to share the heart.

So cherish dreams that softly gleam,
For life is but a fleeting dream.
In crystal hues, we find our way,
With every breath, a new ballet.

Silent Footprints in the White

In silence deep, the snowflakes fall,
A blanket pure, covering all.
With every step, the world holds still,
Entwined in peace, a winter thrill.

Footprints soft on frosted ground,
In the hush, a magic found.
Each mark a story, whispered low,
In white-clad realms where echoes flow.

The trees adorned in crystal grace,
Stand like sentinels, time and space.
While winter's breath, so calm and bright,
Wraps the world in soft twilight.

Beneath the stars, the silence sings,
Of hidden paths and wandering things.
In every breath, a trace remains,
Of whispered dreams and soft refrains.

So walk the white with hearts alight,
In every step, find pure delight.
Silent footprints, a tale anew,
In the snowy realm, just me and you.

The Luminescence of Frosted Thoughts

In the dawn's glow, ideas bloom,
Painted softly in winter's room.
With frosted breath, the mind takes flight,
Illuminating the shadowed night.

Each thought a spark, a glowing thread,
Woven gently with words unsaid.
In icy whispers, visions clear,
The luminescence draws us near.

Through chilly air, the essence flows,
A tapestry where wisdom grows.
Each frosty breath, a moment caught,
In the realm of what we sought.

The winter's hush, a sacred space,
Where thoughts collide and find their place.
A light emerges, fragile yet bold,
In the frost, our stories told.

So let us bask in frosted light,
In every thought, a spark ignites.
For in our minds, the magic glows,
In frosted dreams, our spirit flows.

Ghostly Frontiers of the Whispering Wind

In the stillness, shadows drift,
Softly tracing paths of mist.
Echoes dance on the night breeze,
Where silence holds the moon's kiss.

Whispers tell of secrets lost,
In realms where memories lie.
Voices rise in haunting tones,
As phantoms weave through the sky.

Misty figures in twilight glow,
Bound by time, they silently roam.
Glimmers of worlds not yet shown,
Their stories linger, like the foam.

Each gust speaks of dreams unmet,
Of wanderers who once tread.
In the hollow of the night,
The ghostly frontiers spread.

So listen close to the breeze's call,
For it carries tales of all.
On the edge of the twilight's gleam,
The whispers weave their timeless dream.

Echoes of Breath in the Crystal Air

In the chill of morning's light,
Breath hangs like fragile lace.
Crystal cities built in silence,
Reflecting nature's grace.

Each exhale a fleeting song,
Carried softly by the chill.
Resonating through the trees,
Inspire the heart to fill.

Windswept sounds of voices past,
Intertwined in dreams we share.
Softly sung by sky and earth,
In the crystal-laden air.

Gentle whispers, bold and bright,
Join the dance of frost and glow.
Their echoes stretch, in timeless flight,
Reflecting all that we know.

As the sun begins to rise,
The world awakens with a sigh.
Echoes of breath, crystal clear,
In the embrace of the sky.

Whispers of Frost upon the Wind

Frosty fingers brush the ground,
In the hush of winter's breath.
Whispers twirl on the chill air,
Of stories born from death.

Each flake a whisper, soft and light,
Drifting down from heights so grand.
Silent tales of the night's embrace,
Glisten in the frost-kissed land.

Trees wear coats of shimmering white,
Their branches bending low.
Whispers speak of long-lost warmth,
As fleeting winds do blow.

In this realm of quiet dreams,
Time dances slow and sweet.
Nature's breath, a pure refrain,
In frost's embrace, we meet.

Let the whispers guide the heart,
Through the stillness, through the night.
Frost upon the wind shall sing,
Of beauty wrapped in light.

Harmony of the Shivering Seasons

Autumn leaves in swirling dance,
Compose a symphony of change.
Each color sings of warmth and loss,
In tones that feel so strange.

Winter's breath, a cold refrain,
Crystals sparkle, pure and bright.
The world is wrapped in silent peace,
As day succumbs to night.

Then spring arrives, a gentle hand,
Awakens blooms with tender care.
Nature hums in sweet delight,
With fragrances in the air.

Summer's laughter, warm and bold,
Wraps the world in golden rays.
Crops grow tall, with stories told,
In the sun's eternal blaze.

Together, seasons weave their song,
A harmony, vast and wide.
Through every shift, they carry on,
In nature's dance, we abide.

Frigid Harmony in the Landscape

Snowflakes dance upon the breeze,
Trees stand tall, their branches freeze.
Winter's breath, a gentle sigh,
Painting white beneath the sky.

Softly falls the twilight shade,
In the stillness, warmth displayed.
Footprints trace a tale untold,
Chilled by whispers, brave yet bold.

Silence hums a tranquil tune,
Moonlight bathes the world in rune.
Stars above in icy glow,
Guide the lost where few will go.

Frosty fields where shadows creep,
Nature's secrets, safe to keep.
Crystals gleam, the night is bright,
Embracing all in winter's light.

In this realm so pure and clear,
Hearts beat strong, yet filled with fear.
Frigid harmonies unite,
Beneath the silver stars of night.

Icebound Whispers of a Dream

A frozen lake, a whispered glance,
In the stillness, shadows dance.
Echoes of a distant song,
Where the ice-bound feelings belong.

Dreams reflect in crystal holds,
Winter's heart, stories unfold.
Glimmers bright in twilight's haze,
Chilling winds weave dreams that blaze.

Silvery nights, a haunting call,
Starlit grounds where lovers fall.
Holding tight what time has shared,
In the frost, all feelings bared.

Through the mists of winter's breath,
Hope is born, defying death.
Icebound whispers, softly spoken,
In this realm, no hearts are broken.

As nature rests in deep repose,
Sprightly winds caress the snows.
In dreams unspoken, we take flight,
Chasing warmth through endless night.

The Lure of Winter's Solitude

Lonely roads in silver dress,
Echoing the silent press.
Each step speaks in breathless air,
Wrapped in snow, without a care.

Off the beaten path I tread,
Nature's song, a whisper spread.
Hushed surroundings, time stands still,
Every moment, nature's thrill.

Frosty branches, draped in white,
Stars ignite the velvet night.
In this stillness, thoughts take flight,
Finding spark in winter's light.

Cold embrace, a friend so true,
In solitude, I find the view.
Winding paths through glades unseen,
Nature's brush paints every scene.

In the chill, my spirit sways,
Reflecting on these frozen days.
The lure of winter calls me near,
Embracing peace, forever clear.

Carried Away by the Chill

Under clouds of slate and grey,
Frozen rivers guide my way.
Carried off, a subtle thrill,
In the arms of winter's chill.

Winds that whisper secrets bold,
Softly touch the dreams I hold.
Through the still and icy air,
Nature's magic lingers there.

Drifting softly, snowflakes weave,
In their dance, I dare believe.
Carried on the frosty breeze,
Every moment, heart's unease.

Crisp as morning, bright as stars,
Life spills forth, despite the scars.
Wrapped in layers, we are whole,
Chilled but free, a warming soul.

Each new dawn brings hope undone,
In the chill, we find the sun.
Carried ever, hearts entwined,
In winter's grasp, serenity find.

The Quiet of the Icebound

In the stillness where cold winds blow,
Frozen echoes in pure white glow,
Silent trees dressed in icy lace,
Nature pauses in a tranquil space.

Footsteps muffled on snow's embrace,
Crystal worlds in a gentle trace,
Whispers carried on the chill air,
An untouched beauty, rare and fair.

The sun dips low, a fleeting gleam,
Casting shadows, a winter dream,
Breath condenses in frosty sighs,
Underneath the vast, cerulean skies.

Beneath the ice, life stirs awake,
Roots entwined in the ground they stake,
Awaiting spring's warm, gentle call,
Finding strength beneath the frost's thrall.

In the quiet, deep secrets dwell,
Nature whispers its fragile spell,
Time stands still, a peaceful pause,
In the heart of the icebound cause.

Whispers of a Shivering Heart

In the night when shadows creep,
Silent thoughts begin to seep,
A fragile pulse, a tender ache,
Yearning for warmth, a path to make.

Each heartbeat echoes soft and low,
Whispers in the dark do flow,
A love that dances just out of reach,
Lessons that silence cannot teach.

Eyes close tight against the chill,
Hope flickers like a candle's will,
Embers buried deep in the frost,
In the quiet, nothing is lost.

Dreams take flight on the brittle air,
Woven tightly with tender care,
A shivering heart learning to trust,
Building strength from the frozen dust.

Let the whispers carry me home,
In the stillness, I will roam,
Searching for the warmth I crave,
In the depths, I find my brave.

Withering Warmth

Time drips low like melting ice,
Moments fade in a slow vice,
Once bright embers dimmed to gray,
A fire's glow, now lost away.

Touch once tender, now feels cold,
Stories shared, but none retold,
A gentle warmth slips through my hands,
In the silence, a heart understands.

The sun retreats behind dark clouds,
A lonely weight, my spirit shrouds,
The fading light, a mournful sigh,
As withering warmth wishes goodbye.

Memories linger like a soft haze,
Transformation wrapped in a maze,
Finding solace in what was bright,
Holding on through the creeping night.

Yet in the twilight, hope is spun,
Withering warmth can still be fun,
For every chill has a time to thaw,
In the heart remains a lingering awe.

Silence in Crystal Form

The world outside is a glimmering sheet,
Shimmering crystals beneath my feet,
Every step a soft refrain,
A beauty locked in icy chain.

In this silence, secrets unfold,
Stories simmering, untold gold,
Nature speaks in hushed tones bright,
In crystal form, under the light.

Branches bow with a sparkling weight,
Harmony rests, a tranquil state,
The sound of stillness fills the air,
In this place, only peace to share.

A frozen breath held up high,
Mirrored skies where the angels fly,
Each heartbeat echoes through the frost,
Moments cherished, never lost.

There is magic in this cold embrace,
Capturing time in a timeless space,
In silence, a chorus of the pure,
In crystal form, forever endure.

Frosty Flickers of Time Past

In the twilight glow we stand,
Memories dance like grains of sand.
Whispers of frost weave through the air,
Echoes of laughter linger there.

Time drifts softly, like snowflakes fall,
Each moment captured, a solemn call.
Frozen glimpses of days gone by,
In moonlit shadows, the heart can sigh.

A tapestry woven with threads of light,
Each flicker a tale, both tender and bright.
As seasons change, we hold them dear,
These frosty moments, forever near.

Crystal patterns on window panes,
Nature's artistry, a silent refrain.
Glimmers of past in the present's sway,
Frosty flickers that never decay.

In the quiet night, we find our way,
Through memories cherished, come what may.
With every breath, the past we trace,
In frosty flickers, we find our place.

Silent Notes of a Winter Song

When winter wraps the world in white,
Softly it sings through the starry night.
Each flake a note, a gentle tune,
Whispering secrets beneath the moon.

Branch and bough adorned with grace,
Nature's symphony in every space.
Hushed the day, as shadows blend,
Silent notes that never end.

The rustling wind, a soothing balm,
In quiet moments, the heart feels calm.
Nature's choir sings low and sweet,
In winter's song, our souls entreat.

Frozen rivers hold the heart's refrain,
Melodies drift like soft falling rain.
In every breath, the season sings,
Winter's embrace, our spirit clings.

Listen closely to the winter's call,
Each note a promise, capturing all.
Silent notes in the stillness flow,
Winter's song, a timeless glow.

Breath of the Snowy Veil

A breath of winter cloaks the ground,
In whispered secrets, peace is found.
Softly it sweeps the world away,
With snowy veils at the break of day.

Footprints lost in the quiet white,
Tracing paths through the soft moonlight.
Each gentle flake a fleeting kiss,
A breath of chill, a moment's bliss.

Trees stand tall, draped in snow,
Guardians of dreams where the cold winds blow.
In the silence, stories arise,
The breath of winter, a sweet surprise.

Shadows dance under starlit skies,
With every gust, a soft sigh flies.
Nature whispers in frosty breath,
Wrapped in tranquility, life from death.

A canvas painted in shades of gray,
The snowy veil holds night at bay.
In winter's arms, we find our rest,
In the breath of snow, we are blessed.

Celestial Chills Over the Landscape

Beneath the stars, a chill descends,
Celestial whispers as night extends.
The land is draped in silver light,
A dreamscape born from the winter's night.

Mountains wear crowns of icy sheen,
Nature's art in a tranquil scene.
Each breath a cloud in the crisp night air,
Celestial chills that linger there.

Moonbeams brush the sleeping fields,
Magic within the night time yields.
Frozen rivers beg to reflect,
The dreams and hopes that we protect.

Stars twinkle softly like distant eyes,
Hidden wonders beneath the skies.
In hushed awe, we pause to stare,
Celestial chills that fill the air.

Awakening dawn paints the horizon,
As night retreats, a new day calls on.
Yet in the heart, those chills remain,
A whisper of night, sweet and plain.

The Coolness of Forgotten Hues

In twilight's gentle embrace,
Shadows blend in softest grace.
Whispers of the past collide,
Muted tones in twilight hide.

A palette lost in time's sweet hold,
Stories painted, none retold.
Each shade a memory's breath,
A dance of life, a song of death.

The coolness lingers, sweet and clear,
Echoes of laughter, tracing near.
Fragments lost in fading light,
Colors soft as the coming night.

With every hue, a tale untold,
Lives entwined, like threads of gold.
In corners where the silence grew,
The world sleeps in forgotten hues.

So pause awhile in twilight's glow,
Let the memories softly flow.
The coolness of these shades we find,
A fleeting glimpse of the intertwined.

Nature's Icy Serenity

In winter's breath, the stillness sighs,
A blanket white with open skies.
Crystal branches, gently bow,
Nature's peace, a solemn vow.

The world asleep in gentle frost,
Beauty found in what is lost.
Snowflakes dance on silent winds,
A calm where every heartbeat thins.

Mountains high, cloaked in white,
Whispers soft under pale moonlight.
Serenity in icy embrace,
Time stands still in this sacred space.

Beneath the stars, the earth holds tight,
A tranquil hush, the heart takes flight.
Nature's song, a lullaby,
Echoes sweet beneath the sky.

In every flake, a world reborn,
In icy silence, life is sworn.
A tapestry of cold and grace,
Nature's heart, a still, safe place.

Glaciers Whispering Secrets

Ancient giants, proud and cold,
Guarding stories yet untold.
In crevices, secrets dwell,
Echoes of a frozen swell.

The blue of ice, a dreamlike hue,
Timeless tales that whisper true.
Cracking sounds like voices call,
Nature's chorus, vast and tall.

As glaciers move, a slow ballet,
Carving earth, their regal sway.
Tales of time in every shard,
Glaciers keep their thoughts unmarred.

In frozen depths, a history,
Nature's memory, an endless sea.
With every flow, a truth to find,
In this ice, the past is lined.

So heed the whispers, soft and near,
Listen close, let the stillness steer.
For in their forms, the secrets lie,
Glaciers speak, beneath the sky.

A Symphony of the Chill

Winter winds weave their own tune,
A crisp serenade by the moon.
Each breath a note, each flake a sound,
In silence, melodies abound.

The rustling leaves, a gentle sigh,
Nature's rhythm, soaring high.
Echoes dance on frosty air,
A symphony beyond compare.

Icicles hanging, chimes of light,
Creating music with the night.
A fleeting dance of cold and grace,
Cascading notes in this vast space.

The mountains join, their quiet roar,
In harmony, they sing of yore.
A chill that warms the beating heart,
In this concert, we are a part.

So listen close, let the chill enthrall,
In every note, a winter's call.
A symphony that haunts the mind,
In the deep chill, true peace we find.

Puffs of Ice on the Horizon

Puffs of ice on the distant sea,
Whispers of frost in the morning glee.
Clouds of white stretch wide and free,
Touching the sky, where dreams could be.

Glistening patterns dance in the light,
Crystallized visions, pure and bright.
Every breath a shimmering flight,
In hopes entwined with winter's night.

Fleeting shadows glide on the shore,
Echoes of magic, forevermore.
The horizon beckons, a silent score,
As nature whispers, we long to explore.

Beneath the chill, the world stands still,
As time itself bends to winter's will.
In icy silence, hearts to fill,
With dreams wrapped softly, a quiet thrill.

So let the puffs of ice draw near,
Filling our souls with joy sincere.
In frozen realms, we hold dear,
The beauty of winter, crystal clear.

The Quiet of Subzero Nights

The quiet falls on subzero nights,
Stars awaken, with shimmering lights.
Moonlit shadows play soft sights,
In the hush, the heart ignites.

Snowflakes twirl in the cold embrace,
Each one unique, a delicate lace.
Stillness cradles this sacred space,
Where dreams are spun with gentle grace.

The world a canvas, white and bright,
Whispers of magic in breezes light.
Heartbeats echo in the pale twilight,
Under the gaze of the frosty light.

Branches laden with winter's weight,
Silhouettes dance, as if to sate.
In the void, there's a bond innate,
Embracing stillness, we contemplate.

So breathe in deep the crisp delight,
In the arms of the soft, cold night.
Gather the warmth, hold it tight,
For in this moment, all feels right.

Enchanted Chills of the Forest

Through the woods where silence weaves,
Enchanted chills beneath the leaves.
Frosty fingers touch the eaves,
Nature whispers what it believes.

Moonbeams filter through the trees,
Carving shadows with gentle ease.
In hushed tones, the cold air breathes,
A melody sung by the winter breeze.

Crystals hang like jewels so rare,
Adorning branches with timeless care.
Echoing secrets, a tale to share,
In the stillness, magic lingers there.

Rustling leaves tell stories bold,
Of ancient nights and dreams retold.
With every step, the world unfolds,
A symphony in white and gold.

So wander forth, let the chill embrace,
The forest beckons with gentle grace.
In each breath drawn, find your place,
In nature's heart, a warm embrace.

Veils of Winter's Fancy

Veils of winter drape the land,
Soft as whispers, so gently planned.
Threads of silver in nature's hand,
Creating beauty, vast and grand.

Each flake that falls a dancer's twirl,
In a ballad spun, as dreams unfurl.
Nature's gown, a shimmering pearl,
Inviting all to joyfully swirl.

In the quiet, time slows down,
Fields adorned like a queen's crown.
With every breath, we wear the gown,
Of winter's charm in silver brown.

The evening sky dons hues of blue,
As stars appear for the world to view.
In this silence, our spirits renew,
Wrapped in warmth, beneath the hue.

So let the veils of winter stay,
In our hearts, forever play.
A cherished moment, come what may,
In the frosty magic, we find our way.

Shivering Shadows at Twilight

In the fading light they creep,
Whispers echo, secrets seep.
Dancing forms in gentle gloom,
Silent tales of the night's bloom.

Chill winds trace their ghostly paths,
Breaking stillness with their laughs.
Stars awaken, pale and bright,
Guiding shadows through the night.

Branches sway, a soft ballet,
Nature's music, night's display.
Moonlight weaves through leaves and stone,
Painting dreams in twilight tone.

Caught between the dark and light,
Muffled sounds of fading flight.
Shivers rush down weary spines,
In the dusk, where silence dines.

Twilight whispers, night prevails,
In its arms, all magic sails.
Shivering shadows, softly sway,
Drowning in the night's array.

The Breath of Winter's Embrace

Snowflakes drift on icy breath,
Woven whispers of soft death.
Crisp air bites with tender grace,
Nature wrapped in frosty lace.

Underneath a silver sky,
The world sleeps with a gentle sigh.
Frozen lakes and quiet trails,
Silence stirs where winter wails.

Frosty fingers stretch and twine,
Kissing earth with purest line.
Each crystal spark, a wish cast,
In this moment, time goes fast.

Embers glow in hearth's embrace,
Filling hearts with warmth and space.
As the chill wraps all around,
Love ignites in shadows found.

Winter speaks in hushed tones clear,
Binding souls with hope and cheer.
The breath of ice, a lover's dream,
In the stillness, hearts redeem.

Radiant Crystals of the Cold Night

Twinkling gems on velvet wide,
Each a wish, a tale inside.
Night unfolds with cloak of stars,
Drawing forth the moon's avatars.

Dewy pearls on blades of grass,
Catching light as moments pass.
Whispers float on frosty air,
Magic lives in beauty rare.

A silver path through shadowed trees,
Guided softly by the breeze.
Cold embraces with tender might,
Crystals gleam, a stunning sight.

Every glance sparks tales untold,
Echoes, legends from the cold.
Fractured light in patterns fine,
Radiance from the stars align.

Beneath the hush of endless night,
Dreams are shaped in tranquil light.
Radiant crystals, softly bright,
Jewel of winter's heart and sight.

Subtly Stilled Underneath the Ice

Frozen whispers, time's retreat,
Lies beneath in silent sheet.
Each breath caught in frozen frames,
Nature echoes, softly names.

Buried deep, the earth holds tight,
Secrets kept from day and light.
Frozen rivers, starlit skies,
Breathe in quiet, softly sighs.

Shadows linger, frozen still,
Cracks and creaks give winter's thrill.
Beauty lies where few have trod,
Hidden wonders, nature's god.

Underneath the crystal sheen,
Life is resting, softly keen.
Each heartbeat pulsing deep in frost,
In this stillness, nothing's lost.

Spring will come with thawing grace,
But for now, this sacred space.
Subtly stilled, it waits the sun,
Nature whispers, journeys done.

Fragments of Winter's Heart

Snowflakes dance in the dim light,
Whispers of frost kiss the night.
Brittle branches bend with grace,
Nature sleeps in a silver lace.

Shattered dreams of the autumn past,
Frozen moments, shadows cast.
Memories linger, cold and clear,
Held together, forever near.

Icicles hang like crystal tears,
Silent witnesses to our fears.
Amidst the chill, love's warmth does start,
Binding together, fragments of heart.

Biting winds through the silence flow,
Carrying secrets from deep below.
In winter's embrace, we find our way,
Each heartbeat echoes, none can sway.

Fragments freeze, yet beauty thrives,
In icy realms, our spirit strives.
Winter's breath, a gentle sigh,
From frozen depths, we learn to fly.

Icy Echoes of Silence

In the stillness, frost takes hold,
Echoes whisper, stories told.
Moonlight glimmers on frozen streams,
Chasing shadows from our dreams.

Windswept valleys, vast and white,
Shrouded in the veil of night.
Each breath a ghost beneath the sky,
Crystals shimmer as time slips by.

Hushed is the world, lost in peace,
Nature revels in sweet release.
Footsteps crunch on the icy ground,
A melody of winter's sound.

Stars above, like diamonds rare,
Glimpse of warmth in the cold air.
Icy echoes blend with dreams,
As silence reigns, so it seems.

Through frozen woods, a soft embrace,
Life holds its breath, a sacred space.
In the still of night, we find our way,
Icy echoes that forever stay.

Breath of the Arctic Night

Under the blanket of endless stars,
Whispers of the night heal our scars.
The arctic breath, crisp and profound,
Where secrets of the universe abound.

Glistening fields of purest white,
Wrapped in the cradle of soft twilight.
As silence envelops the moonlit glow,
Shadows play, dances slow.

Frost-kissed air, a sparkling sigh,
Time hangs still as the moments fly.
Every heartbeat, a distant call,
Under the heavens, we rise, we fall.

In the expanse, our spirits soar,
Breath of the night, forevermore.
Each glimmering star, a story spun,
In the vastness, we become one.

From the arctic deep, we draw our strength,
Writing our tales in the night's vast length.
With every sigh and every glance,
Breath of the night, our timeless dance.

Shivers Beneath the Stars

Cold winds beckon, a shiver deep,
Underneath the stars, we leap.
Flickers of light in the velvet sea,
Each twinkle whispers, 'Come away with me.'

The frost lays its claim on the ground,
Nature's canvas, a beauty profound.
With every gaze into night's embrace,
Find solace in the hidden space.

Beneath the heavens, we find our home,
In chilly air, we are free to roam.
Each constellation tells a tale,
Of hope and dreams that gently sail.

Echoes of laughter in the quiet night,
In the chill, our souls take flight.
Creating warmth in the freezing air,
Together we dance, shedding our care.

Stars our witnesses, the moon our guide,
Shivers shared, hearts open wide.
In the depths of winter, love persists,
Beneath the stars, we find our bliss.

Shards of Light in December's Grip

In the hush of falling snow,
Sunbeams dance, a soft glow.
Frosted branches lightly sway,
Whispering secrets of the day.

Glints of silver on the ground,
Nature's beauty, lost yet found.
Each flake tells a fleeting tale,
Beneath the winter's icy veil.

Footprints mark the silent scene,
Memory woven, pure and clean.
Time stands still, as shadows creep,
In December's grip, dreams sleep.

Beyond the chill, a fire's light,
Stories shared on long, cold nights.
Embers glow with warmth so bright,
As we embrace the tranquil night.

Hope glimmers in the frosty air,
Shards of light, a gentle flare.
From winter's grasp, we long to break,
Creating warmth from the heart's ache.

Celestial Coldness in Twilight

Stars awaken in the night,
Drawing patterns, pure delight.
Moonbeams brush the silent ground,
Celestial coldness all around.

Whispers echo through the trees,
Carried softly by the breeze.
Frosted petals glisten bright,
In the stillness of twilight.

Crimson skies begin to fade,
As shadows lengthen, softly laid.
Nature dons her evening gown,
In the twilight's gentle crown.

The world beneath a silken dome,
Each heartbeat finds its way back home.
Underneath the stars we dream,
In the quiet, all is serene.

Celestial beauty paints the night,
As we find warmth in cold's bite.
In the calm, a promise lies,
That dawn will break the darkened skies.

The Lament of the Winter Sky

A blanket gray drapes the morn,
In the hush, a heart is torn.
Clouds like whispers, soft but low,
Weaving tales of winter's woe.

Frozen tears from heavens fall,
In silence, nature hears the call.
The wind carries a mournful tune,
Underneath the watchful moon.

Branches bare, stripped of song,
Yearning for the light so long.
Echoes of a bright summer's day,
Linger where the shadows lay.

Stars, hidden behind the veil,
Lost in sorrow, thin and pale.
Yet the promise of rebirth stays,
Awaiting spring's warm embrace.

In the lament, the stillness sings,
Of hope that each new season brings.
Though winter's grasp is cold and tight,
Life ebbs softly, out of sight.

Breathless Beneath a Blanket of Ice

Silence swathes the frozen ground,
In this stillness, no sound found.
Breathless under icy sheet,
Nature rests, serene and sweet.

Each flake falls like whispered dreams,
Draped in silver, soft moonbeams.
Frosted whispers, crisp and clear,
In the stillness, we draw near.

A world transformed by winter's hand,
Glorious, yet vast and grand.
In the chill, we seek the spark,
To light the way through shadows dark.

Frozen lakes, like mirrors show,
Reflections of a fleeting glow.
As night wraps tight, we hold our breath,
In winter's grip, we find our strength.

Amidst the frost, we learn to grow,
In frozen beauty, love will flow.
Breathless here, we find our peace,
Under ice, our hearts release.

Frost-kissed Murmurs

Whispers dance on icy breath,
Veils of white conceal the path,
In the stillness, silence lies,
Nature's quilt in quiet sighs.

Crisp air carries tales untold,
Frozen secrets in the cold,
Every flake a fragile dream,
Caught beneath the moon's soft gleam.

Branches stretch like ancient arms,
Cradling night's enchanting charms,
Sparkling edges catch the light,
A world transformed in muted white.

Footsteps crunch on frozen ground,
Echoes of the night surround,
With every step, a story grows,
In the frost, the magic flows.

As dawn breaks on the frosted morn,
Colors rise, a day reborn,
Yet, still the whispers gently play,
Frost-kissed murmurs fade away.

Chilling Exhalations

In the breath of winter's chill,
Every exhale sharp and still,
Frosted air, a biting kiss,
Nature's frozen, tranquil bliss.

Clouds of white drift softly down,
Wrapping earth in icy gown,
Each inhalation sparks a dream,
Of warmth found in the quiet stream.

Branches bare against the sky,
Shivers dance as spirits fly,
Chilling echoes fill the space,
In this hushed, enchanted place.

Time slows down in frosty air,
Every moment rich and rare,
With each puff a story told,
In the heart, the warmth takes hold.

As twilight comes to claim the light,
Stars emerge, a shimmering sight,
Chilling exhalations weave around,
In the night, lost dreams are found.

Echoes of Frigid Dreams

In the depths where shadows creep,
Frigid dreams begin to seep,
Whispers low beneath the frost,
Memories of the warmth we lost.

Every sigh a haunting call,
In the stillness, echoes fall,
Winds carry tales of the past,
Fleeting moments meant to last.

Underneath the frozen veil,
A world slumbers, soft and pale,
Crystals form in muted glow,
Reflecting all the dreams we know.

Each glimmer holds a wish so dear,
Fading softly, yet so near,
As the nights grow long and deep,
In our hearts, the echoes keep.

When the dawn breathes life anew,
Frigid dreams begin to strew,
But the echoes will remain,
Dancing softly in the brain.

Shattered Frost on Glass

Morning breaks with a soft crack,
Nature whispers, no turning back,
Shattered frost on window pane,
Artistry from night's domain.

In each shard, a story hides,
Twisted tales where beauty bides,
Delicate patterns, lace-like grace,
Captured moments time can't erase.

Breathless marvel at the sight,
Sunrise spills its golden light,
Transforming ice to glistening haze,
Painting dreams in warming rays.

Each fragment glows with history,
Echoes of a winter mystery,
Shattered frost, a fleeting dance,
Nature's splendor, pure romance.

As the day unfolds ahead,
Windows clear, the frost will shed,
Yet in the heart, it leaves a mark,
Of shattered frost and morning's spark.

Ribbons of Ice in the Morning Light

Morning breaks with tender grace,
Ribbons of ice in a warm embrace.
Glistening whispers on branches sway,
A soft ballet where dawn holds sway.

Sunrise paints a canvas bright,
Reflecting gems in pure delight.
Gentle winds weave through the trees,
Nature's breath, a whispered tease.

Each crystal glows with stories old,
Silent tales of winter told.
A fleeting moment, frozen tight,
Ribbons of ice in the morning light.

As shadows dance and daylight wakes,
In the stillness, the cold heart aches.
Yet hope springs forth; the world feels new,
In every sparkle, a fresh view.

A tapestry spun of frost and sun,
In harmony, the day's begun.
Each fleeting second, a precious sight,
Ribbons of ice in the morning light.

The Song of the Sighing Frost

When twilight falls and stars ignite,
The song of frost takes graceful flight.
Beneath the moon's soft silver hue,
Echoes linger in the night's view.

Crisp air carries a haunting tune,
A melody born from the cold of June.
Whispers rise from the frozen ground,
In every sigh, the night is crowned.

Blankets of snow hush the earth,
Silent serenades of wintry mirth.
Each flake dances, a gentle sweep,
In the arms of night, they softly weep.

A shiver runs through the chilly breeze,
Nature's breath whispers with ease.
Songs of silence, soft and lost,
In harmony, the sighing frost.

As dawn approaches, the chorus fades,
Yet in our hearts, the music wades.
A whispered promise, forever tossed,
In dreams we'll sing with the sighing frost.

Layers of Silence in the Air

Silent blankets drape the trees,
Whispers float on the wintry breeze.
Layers of silence, thick and deep,
In the heart of the world, secrets keep.

Frost-kissed branches arch with care,
Holding the hush of the still, cold air.
Each breath lingers, a moment long,
In the quiet, nature's song.

Snowflakes drift from skies above,
Wrapping the earth in a quiet glove.
Each layer holds a touch of grace,
Embracing the chill in a soft embrace.

The world outside is a muted hue,
A canvas white, a tranquil view.
In the layers of silence, peace we find,
In a frozen moment, hearts unwind.

As evening falls, shadows grow near,
In the stillness, all we hold dear.
Layers of silence, time stands bare,
In winter's grasp, we breathe the air.

Shadows of Winter's Lament

In the dusk where shadows play,
Winter sings, in soft decay.
A haunting echo, deep and low,
In the silence, memories flow.

Bare trees stretch against the sky,
Whispering secrets of days gone by.
Frosty sighs in the twilight's grasp,
In every breath, the cold winds clasp.

Footprints linger on the snow,
Stories told where cold winds blow.
A sigh escapes from the frozen ground,
In winter's heart, soft lament is found.

Each shadow dances, a fleeting shade,
Carving paths where dreams once played.
A tapestry of dark and light,
In the depths of the frigid night.

Yet spring will come, with tender hands,
To brush away the winter's strands.
But until then, we heed the chant,
Of shadows soft in winter's lament.

Slumbering Echoes on the Edge of Night

In shadows deep, the whispers flow,
Dreams entwine where soft winds blow.
A lullaby of starlit air,
Cradles thoughts that drift and dare.

Each heartbeat fades, a gentle song,
In twilight's grasp, we all belong.
Echoes stir with the night's embrace,
Finding solace in this space.

Moonbeams dance on silken sheets,
In slumbered realms, the heart still beats.
A voyage through the quiet dark,
Where whispered hopes ignite a spark.

Fingers trace the dreams we keep,
In the cradle of the deep.
Rest now, dear, let worries cease,
As night enfolds you, granting peace.

Through the mist, the echoes sigh,
A serenade beneath the sky.
Sleep and dream, let shadows play,
Till dawn breaks forth and steals away.

Frigid Reflections upon the Soul

A mirror held to frozen days,
Where shadows dance in silvered ways.
The chill wraps close, a tender knit,
In silence deep, our souls must sit.

Thoughts cascade like falling snow,
Each flake a truth we dare not show.
In icy grips, our fears unfold,
The heart concealed, the mind grown cold.

In stillness, whispers find their place,
Fragile light, but fierce in grace.
Through bitter winds, we search and seek,
A warmth that blooms in words we speak.

Reflections glint like distant stars,
Healing wounds that leave their scars.
In frosty breath, the spirit yearns,
For fire's touch, as winter churns.

Yet every silence sings its tune,
A melody beneath the moon.
In frigid nights, our souls can heal,
Finding strength in what we feel.

Among the Snowflakes' Whisper

In gentle fall, the snowflakes weave,
A tapestry, the heart can cleave.
Each flake a story, pure and bright,
Whispers of winter take their flight.

Among the drifts, the silence reigns,
Softly brushing away the pains.
Crystals glisten in soft twilight,
Calling forth the magic of night.

Intricate patterns upon the ground,
In every swirl, a joy is found.
Frost-kissed dreams twirl in the air,
As laughter echoes everywhere.

The world transformed; a quiet grace,
Each flake a wonder, time can't erase.
Through winter's breath, we learn to see,
Beauty in all that strives to be.

So let us dance among the white,
And lose ourselves in pure delight.
For in this hush, we are set free,
Among the snowflakes, you and me.

The Dance of the Frosted Pines

Beneath the boughs of frosted green,
A chorus of the still unseen.
The pines sway gently in the breeze,
Their whispered secrets flow with ease.

A ballet borne on winter's breath,
In nature's pause, embraces death.
Yet life persists, through crystal skies,
In every sway, a spirit flies.

The moonlit glow, a guiding light,
Drapes the forest in silvered white.
Together, roots and branches twine,
In harmony, the sacred shrine.

With every gust, the echoes call,
The dance unfolds, a soft enthrall.
Fragrant scents of pine and frost,
In this embrace, no love is lost.

So let the night eternal play,
While frosted pines in grandeur sway.
In tranquil breaths, our hearts align,
To share in nature's grand design.

Echoes of Frigid Laughter

In the quiet woods, laughter fades,
Whispers of joy in icy braids.
Snowflakes dance on the silent breeze,
Echoes linger among the trees.

Memories wrapped in a frost-kissed glow,
Where shadows play and moonlight flows.
Frigid joy, a fleeting spark,
Glints beneath the winter dark.

Through the frosty air, voices ring,
Chasing warmth that chill can bring.
Echoes swirl like the falling snow,
In the hush of night, they come and go.

Laughter lingers, a spectral sound,
In the stillness, it wraps around.
Frosted dreams on a winter night,
Breathe in the chill, hold tight to light.

In this realm where time is still,
Every echo brings a thrill.
With each cold breath, we softly sigh,
Frigid laughter will never die.

Frost-laden Verses of the Soul

In the stillness, whispers tread,
Frosty verses left unsaid.
Each breath, a cloud in the night,
Painting dreams in silver light.

Cold fingers trace the frozen glass,
Carving tales of fragile past.
With every sigh, a story flows,
A dance of life where the cold wind blows.

In shivers, warmth hides within,
Echoes of laughter, we begin.
Frost-laden thoughts, so clear, so bright,
Illuminate the endless night.

Snowfall blankets the silent ground,
In this stillness, peace is found.
A tapestry of winter's grace,
Enfolds our hearts in its embrace.

Chilled emotions, tender and raw,
Weaving feelings with every thaw.
With every verse, the world unrolls,
Frost-laden dreams awaken souls.

Breathless Moments in Chill

In the crispness of the dawn,
Breathless moments quietly drawn.
Caught in whispers of the air,
Chilled sensations linger there.

Every heartbeat, a frozen mist,
Moments spark that can't be missed.
Winter's breath, a subtle tease,
Melodies in the rustling leaves.

Glistening paths of powdered snow,
Lead us where the soft winds blow.
Each step measured, slow but sure,
In the chill, our spirits soar.

As twilight falls, the world stands still,
Breathless echoes that fate will fill.
In quietude, our hearts entwine,
In icy realms, love's warmth aligns.

Through breathless moments, time will bend,
In winter's chill, we transcend.
With each exhale, we softly find,
Treasures of the heart defined.

A Dance of White upon the Breath

Dancing softly, snowflakes fall,
Whispers of white, a beckoning call.
Each flake twirls in the moonlit air,
A ballet of silence, beauty rare.

With every breath, the world transforms,
Into quiet realms where magic warms.
A fleeting glimpse of winter's song,
Where hearts are light, and souls belong.

Caught in the grip of winter's charm,
Where laughter lingers, a soothing balm.
A dance of white upon our lips,
Soft-kissed moments, sweet winter trips.

Through the shadows, frosty sights,
The landscape glows in silver nights.
With each exhale, a dream takes flight,
A symphony of chilly light.

In this dance, we find our way,
Guided by stars that gently sway.
A tender chill wraps us tight,
In winter's embrace, we find delight.

Melodies of the Cold

In the hush of frost-kissed air,
Notes of silence linger there.
Bare branches sway with a sigh,
Echoes of winter pass by.

Snowflakes dance in the pale moon,
A soft embrace, a gentle tune.
Whispers trace the icy ground,
In this stillness, peace is found.

Stars peek through the velvet night,
Warming hearts with distant light.
Fires crackle, shadows gleam,
A cozy, shared winter dream.

Melodies float on the breeze,
Stirring memories, with such ease.
Winter's charm, a timeless flow,
In every flake, a story grows.

Wrapped in layers, snug and tight,
We find joy in the long night.
With each note, our spirits rise,
As winter sings beneath the skies.

Bated Whispers of Winter

Whispers soft as the falling snow,
Creeping slowly, quiet and low.
Winter's breath on cheeks so red,
Tales of warmth that dreams have fed.

Branches bare in ghostly grace,
Nature's canvas in a frozen space.
Each flake tells a tale unheard,
As silence falls, like a whispered word.

Footsteps crunch on the icy path,
Chasing shadows, feeling the aftermath.
The world transformed, a wonderland,
In this stillness, hand in hand.

Starlit skies in the early eve,
Wrapped in silence, we believe.
Moments linger, time stands still,
With every breath, we chase our thrill.

The night unfolds its velvet cloak,
In its presence, hearts invoke.
Whispers fade as dreams take flight,
In the calm of winter's night.

Frigid Lullabies at Dusk

As day succumbs to twilight's touch,
The world grows quiet, still, and such.
Frigid lullabies begin to play,
Cradling thoughts as night holds sway.

Moonlight dances upon the ground,
In a realm where peace is found.
Wrapped in blankets, stories unfold,
Each moment cherished, warmth untold.

Breath of fog, a ghostly sight,
In the hush of the falling night.
Stars blink softly, a gentle nod,
Guiding dreams on a snowy trod.

Frosty windows, a canvas bright,
Adorned with nature's purest light.
As winter's song weaves through the air,
Lullabies echo, casting care.

In this twilight, hearts align,
With whispers sweet and sips of wine.
Frigid dreams on the edge of dusk,
Embracing warmth, in love we trust.

A Song of Winter's Breath

Winter's breath sings through the pines,
A melody in nature's lines.
Chill of air, a crisp refrain,
Echoes softly in the brain.

Breathless moments caught in time,
A song of nature, pure and prime.
Frosted whispers dance and glide,
In a world that swells with pride.

Each flake drifting is a note,
On winter's staff, they gently float.
Harmony in every breeze,
An orchestra of frosted trees.

As night falls, shadows creep,
In this stillness, secrets keep.
Moon above, a guiding light,
Illuminates the quiet night.

Voices rise in joyful cheer,
Winter's song, so sweet and clear.
In every heart, a fire glows,
As winter whispers, love it sows.

Dreams Encased in Ice

In the stillness of night, dreams glide,
Encased in ice, where hopes abide.
Whispers of winter, soft and light,
Shimmering visions in the pale moonlight.

Chill winds carry tales of old,
Frozen secrets waiting, bold.
In the frost, a story unfolds,
Of dreams entwined in glimmering gold.

Through the glassy silence, thoughts drift near,
Caught in the brume of the atmosphere.
Threads of ambition, woven tight,
Beneath the stars in the frosty night.

Each breath a cloud, a fleeting trace,
Memories captured in frozen embrace.
Dancing shadows on the ice's face,
In this world, we find our place.

In dreams encased, we swirl and sway,
Chasing light through the milky way.
Bound in frost till the break of day,
Awakening hope as the ice gives way.

Frigid Fantasia

In a realm where snowflakes weave,
A frigid dance, we can't believe.
Mirrors of ice reflecting glow,
As twilight whispers soft and low.

Fantasy blooms in the frosty air,
With each breath, a dream we share.
Luminous creatures on the gleaming ground,
In their world, warmth's never found.

Snow-laden branches, delicate and bright,
Embracing the chill of the starry night.
Shadows whisper through the silent trees,
In this fantastical winter breeze.

In frigid dreams, we take our flight,
Through the tapestry of purest white.
Waltzing with time, we glide and sway,
In realms where the snowflakes play.

With frosty fingers, we touch the sky,
As clouds above begin to sigh.
In this moment, we transcend,
Frigid fantasia, all hearts mend.

Frosty Reflections and Dreams

Upon the surface, still and clear,
Frosty reflections draw us near.
A world embraced in white and gray,
Where night and day merge in a ballet.

In the glimmer of ice, visions dance,
Like fleeting thoughts in a dream's trance.
Glistening whispers under the stars,
Echoes of secrets from afar.

Each sigh of winter stirs the soul,
In crystal landscapes, we feel whole.
Mirrors to memories lost in the haze,
Frosty reflections in the winter's maze.

In dreams we wander, lost in time,
In the reverie of winter's rhyme.
With every breath, a promise gleams,
In the quietude of frosty dreams.

Here we find solace, here we belong,
Where night whispers soft, a lullaby song.
Frosted visions, a tender embrace,
A world of wonder, a tranquil place.

Echoes of a White Exhalation

In the hush of dawn, a breath appears,
Echoes of a white exhalation, near.
Softly it drapes the slumbering land,
A blanket of purity, cool and grand.

Whispers of winter weave through the day,
Letters of snowflakes in quiet play.
Each flake a promise, unique and bright,
In the ballet of shadow and light.

As daylight fades, colors intertwine,
In a tapestry crafted by design.
Echoes linger in every sigh,
As night descends from a velvet sky.

In the frost's embrace, we come alive,
Where dreams breathe in the chill, we strive.
Moments caught in icy frames,
In shimmering whispers, we find our names.

Through the silence, soft and deep,
Echoes of memories drift and seep.
In the heart of winter's gentle breath,
We find our essence, transcending death.

The Quietude of the Snowbound Heart

In the stillness of the night,
A heart beats soft and slow,
Wrapped in blankets made of dreams,
Where winter's whispers softly flow.

Silent breath of falling snow,
Covers all with gentle grace,
Each flake a sacred secret,
In this still and wondrous space.

Stars peek through the chilly mist,
Their twinkling eyes watch near,
Guiding thoughts like drifting flakes,
In the warmth of quiet cheer.

A frozen world yet alive,
Where echoes softly play,
In the arms of winter's calm,
Guiding souls through night and day.

Here the heart finds peace embraced,
In the breath of frosty air,
With each pulse, the quietude,
Feels the love that lingers there.

Specters of the Icy Wind

Whispers ride on icy gusts,
Carrying tales of old,
Specters dance in silver light,
Through the night, their secrets told.

Beneath the moon's pale gaze,
Shadows trace forgotten paths,
Where echoes blend with chill of air,
In the dark, the cold heart laughs.

With every haunting breath of snow,
Memories swirl like drifting leaves,
Past and present intertwine,
In the spell that winter weaves.

Frigid fingers clutch the trees,
Crystals glimmer, sharp and bright,
Nature's breath, a chilling song,
Enfolded in the cloak of night.

These specters glide without a sound,
Haunting every quiet street,
Where the winter winds conspire,
And chilled hearts embrace defeat.

Ethereal Lullabies in the Cold

A lullaby of crystal tones,
Drifts upon the frozen ground,
In the hush of winter's breath,
Peaceful rhythms can be found.

Softly sung by moonlit skies,
Each note a tender grace,
Wrapping dreams in frosty wraps,
Filling hearts, a warm embrace.

Gentle winds caress the trees,
While stars twinkle, softly sigh,
Whispered hopes on winter's breath,
Ethereal wishes float and fly.

In this cold, a warmth ignites,
Within the stillness of the night,
In each flake that softly falls,
Lies the promise of delight.

Come, let dreams come dancing near,
In the soft embrace of snow,
Ethereal lullabies will sing,
To guide us where love flows.

Frost-kissed Memories of Yesterday

Frost-kissed thoughts from days gone by,
Nestle close like winter's breath,
Wrapped in echoes, soft and clear,
A tapestry of life and Death.

Each shimmering flake a moment,
Silent frozen in our mind,
Glimmers of a vivid past,
In the chill, their warmth we find.

Snowy blankets hold the tales,
Of laughter, love, and faded grace,
In the arms of winter's shroud,
Memories find their rightful place.

Through the cold, the heart recalls,
The joy and sorrow intertwined,
In the frost, a bittersweet,
A tender kiss to love confined.

So here we stand, in quiet night,
Embracing whispers of the past,
Frost-kissed memories linger on,
In dreams, their shadows cast.

Milton Keynes UK
Ingram Content Group UK Ltd.
UKHW010232111224
452348UK00011B/693